The *Spirit*
of the
Oregon
Coast

A Collection of Coastal Images

Suzanne and Bruce Watkins

Published by
Brewster Press
Copyright © 2006
Suzanne and Bruce Watkins

All rights of text and photography are reserved.
No part of this publication may be reproduced, stored in a
retrieval system or transferred by any means or in any form
either electronically, mechanically, or by photocopy without the express written permission of the publisher.

Quotations used throughout this book are the intellectual
property of the acknowledged originators. We hold no
claim of copyright on the individual quotations other than
our own. Use of these quotations are done with the fair
copyright principal at large.

We do claim intellectual property rights including, without
any limitations, copyright on our compilations of these
quotations and their compositional connection to the
unique style of photo positioning and page design of this
book.

First Edition

International Standard Book Number 0-9776879-0-2
Library of Congress Control Number 2005911088

Published in the United States of America
Printed and bound in Hong Kong

Designed and produced by
Suzanne and Bruce Watkins
and Rob O'Lenic • Robert S. O'Lenic Design

Photo Credits:
    USCG Yaquina Bay Station Newport, Oregon:
    • USCG 52 MLB Victory
    • USCG 47 MLB

▶ *View from Cape Blanco to Port Orford.*

▶▶ *Sunset at Driftwood Shores, Florence, Oregon.*

We dedicate this book
to our four children
Mark, Suzy, William and Lisa
and their families…
all of whom have enjoyed with us

The Spirit of The Oregon Coast.

Contents

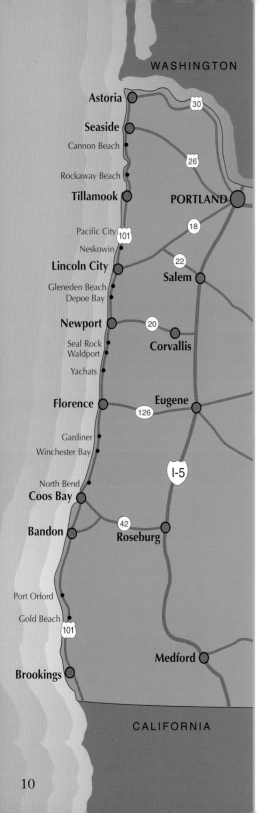

The Spirit of The Oregon Coast

Places should have their own spirit. How else do we recognize their enchantment? Part of the allure of being on the Oregon Coast is letting your eyes follow the waves, observing shifting patterns of sand; watching what makes the coastline stay the same in some places and respond to dynamics of change in others. Then, there is the ocean air - salt spray and refreshingly clean scents. Whatever its attraction; the coast is seductive.

An American Experience

History makes a significant stop on this coast. It is recorded in the books that speak glowingly of the American experience. This is where exploration of land by our forefathers reached its apex in the nineteenth century. Only because of the confrontation with the Pacific Ocean was it the stopping place in young America's quest to secure ownership of the West.

On the Oregon Coast, there is still a future to find, the present to revel in and a past that adheres to old fashioned values. It is the simplicity – straight forwardness and satisfaction with living a life in one of God's great creations.

◄◄ *Rusted bulwark protects the Port of Astoria.*

▲ *Trawler travels up the Columbia River under the Astoria-Megler Bridge.*

▲ *Pelican Bay Lighthouse, one of two privately owned lighthouses on the Oregon Coast, serves as the light to the Port of Brookings Harbor and Pelican Bay. This is at the southernmost point on the Oregon Coast.*

Coast
Bays

Mother Nature put them bays in place so as boats would have safe harbors.
Them bridges were built over 'em so as not to interfere with either of 'em.

- Overheard at Winchester Bay

Blue striped sails reflect on Coos Bay.

▲ *Yaquina Bay Bridge structure at sunset.*

bay (bā)   a body of water forming an indentation of the shoreline, larger than a cove but smaller than a gulf.

boat (bōt)   a vessel for transport by water, propelled by rowing, sails or a motor.

bridge (brij)   a structure spanning and providing passage over a river, chasm, bay, estuary or the like.

▲ *Siuslaw River Bridge at sunset.*

Oregon Coast Bays

- Alsea Bay
- Boiler Bay
- Coos Bay
- Depoe Bay
- Nehalem Bay
- Nestucca Bay
- Netarts Bay
- Siletz Bay
- Sunset Bay
- Tillamook Bay
- Winchester Bay
- Yaquina Bay

Bays and estuaries are a major part of the natural phenomena of the coast. They are the liquid land environment that gives birth and feeding to an abundance of life that thrives in this unique ecological environment.

▲ *Mist shrouds sunrise over Siuslaw River estuary.*

▶ *Boats rest at Coos Bay Boardwalk.*

Yaquina Bay Yacht Club sailing dinghies at the end of the race, floating on their own reflections.

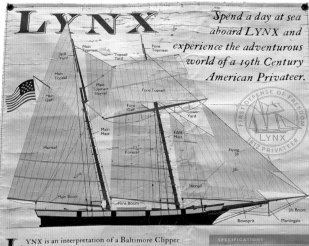

LYNX

Spend a day at sea aboard LYNX and experience the adventurous world of a 19th Century American Privateer.

L YNX is an interpretation of a Baltimore Clipper Schooner from the War of 1812. These two-masted vessels with heavily-raked spars were renowned for their speed, which made them ideal as privateers or naval dispatch schooners.

The original LYNX was built at Fells Point, Maryland in 1812 and captured by the British in 1813. Because of her speed and design, she was taken into the Royal Navy where she was renamed the *Mosquidobit* and based out of Halifax, Nova Scotia.

In keeping with her mission to bring to life the naval traditions of the early 19th century, LYNX has been fitted with historic artillery—four six-pounder carronades and four half-pounder swivel guns—and her crew wears uniforms of the 1812 period.

Charters are available.

SPECIFICATIONS	
Rig	Square Topsail Schooner
Flag	United States of America
Registry	Portsmouth, New Hampshire
U.S. Coast Guard Classification	Passenger Vessel (subchapter T)
Sparred Length	122'
Length Over All	78'
Beam	23'
Draft	9'
Displacement	114 tons
Hull Planking	Angelique
Deck	Douglas Fir
Height of Mainmast	94'
Sail Area	5000 sq.ft.
Masts & Yards	Laminated Douglas Fir
Crew	5
Berths	14
Day Sail Capacity	40
Armament	4 six-pounder carronade
	4 half-pounder swivels
Power	290 h.p. Caterpillar diesel
Owner/Operator	Woods Maritime, LLC
	Newport Beach, California
Designer	Melbourne Smith
	Annapolis, Maryland
Builder	Rockport Marine
	Rockport, Maine
Launched	July 28, 2001 - Rockport, Maine

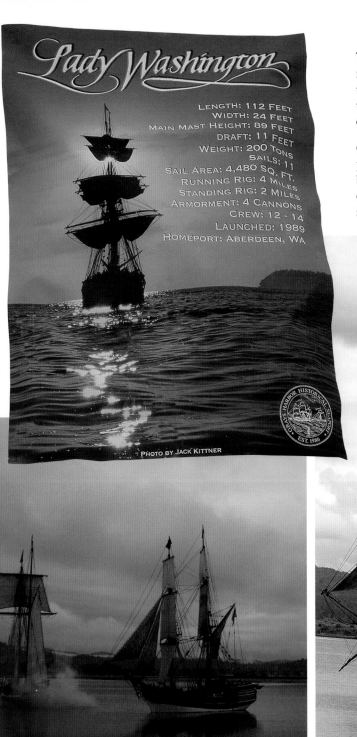

Lady Washington

LENGTH: 112 FEET
WIDTH: 24 FEET
MAIN MAST HEIGHT: 89 FEET
DRAFT: 11 FEET
WEIGHT: 200 TONS
SAILS: 11
SAIL AREA: 4,480 SQ. FT.
RUNNING RIG: 4 MILES
STANDING RIG: 2 MILES
ARMORMENT: 4 CANNONS
CREW: 12 - 14
LAUNCHED: 1989
HOMEPORT: ABERDEEN, WA

PHOTO BY JACK KITTNER

The square-rigged brig Lady Washington is a full scale replica of the first vessel to explore the Pacific Northwest. Sailing together, Lynx and Lady Washington, stage unscripted mock battles while under sail. Spectators were invited aboard for this evening cruise event in Coos Bay.

Crews try to outmaneuver each other while firing cannons using powder charges. "Crossing the T" puts either ship at an advantage bringing fire power to bear at very close range. The objective for each ship is to position themselves broadside across the other vessel's bow or stern.

working fisherman's lament

the mornings come on
and fishing boats are back
some hauls are good and others slack

the fishing is hard
and the work brings pain
is all of this just in vain?

most days are wet with cold
and some days are hot with wet
all of the days are days of sweat

most bunks are much too stiff
and some bunks smell of mold
is this the way to grow old?

we live to work
and we work to live
is this all there is to give?

- Angus B. Campbell

Charter fishing boat returning to Depoe Bay.

▲ Spring wildflowers show off the Siuslaw River Bridge.

Oregon Coast Bridges
North to South

- Astoria-Megler Bridge
- Youngs Bay Bridge
- Lewis and Clark River Bridge
- Necarney Creek Bridge
- Chasm (*Neahkahnie Mtn.*) Bridge
- Wilson River Bridge
- Depoe Bay Bridge
- Rocky Creek Bridge
- Yaquina Bay Bridge
- New Alsea Bay Bridge
- Cummins Creek Bridge
- Tenmile Creek Bridge
- Big Creek Bridge
- Cape Creek Bridge
- Siuslaw River Bridge
- Umpqua River Bridge
- Coos Bay Bridge
- Brush Creek Bridge
- Rogue River Bridge
- Thomas Creek Bridge

Bridges on the Oregon Coast were built to cross over water… rivers, estuaries and bays. Some of the bridges are long; others short. Each bridge serves a universal purpose: Connecting Coast Highway 101.

Astoria-Megler Bridge crossing the Columbia River from Oregon to Washington.

Coast
Beaches

Oregon's Beaches Belong to All of The People.
                        - Tom McCall

... it is in the public interest to do whatever is necessary to preserve and protect scenic and recreational use of Oregon's ocean shore.

- Oregon House Bill 1601- Section 4

f you know the East Coast of the United States and are familiar with the coastline of California then you are aware of how these areas have been overdeveloped. In very few places on the eastern seaboard and in California do the public have access to beaches. But, in Oregon, access has been assured to the public for all time.

How did this come about? One of Oregon's youngest governors at age 37, Oswald West, saw the access issue as one of great importance. In 1913, he initiated legislation that would persuade Oregon lawmakers to declare Oregon's beaches to be public highways.

Years later, Governor Tom McCall continued this call to conservation and signed into law House Bill 1601. It was to be characterized as the Beach Bill. This legislation took place after widespread public outcry against private land grabs in the Cannon Beach area. In 1967, the Beach Bill was signed into law. It was then, and still is, an extraordinary act of conservation on behalf of a deserving public.

Essentially, a brief extrapolation of the House Bill states the law this way:

The Legislative Assembly hereby declares it is the public policy of the State of Oregon to forever preserve and maintain the sovereignty of the state heretofore legally existing over the ocean shore of the state from the Columbia River on the north to the Oregon-California line on the south so that the public may have the free and uninterrupted use thereof.

So, from the forward looking, public-minded Governor Oswald West, who recounted in 1913 how...

"I came up with a bright idea. And this was very much a surprise for I have enjoyed but few of such in a lifetime. I drafted a simple short bill declaring the seashore from the Washington line to California line a public highway. I pointed out that thus we would come into miles and miles of highway without cost to the taxpayer."

The Beach Bill has stood for decades as a landmark of conservation legislation. It shines as an example: *Preservation over development, aesthetics over commercialism.*

A short walk on the beach can cast a long shadow.

A Long Look Down The Beach

Someone once said that you can look so far down the beach that the distance can be measured by a scale of one look away or two looks away. And if the space is wide open and the light is just right, you can see three looks away…which is a very long look down the beach.

▶ *Agate Beach from Yaquina Head Natural Area to Yaquina Bay Bridge.*

You Can Never Step Twice Onto The Same Beach

Oregon Coast beaches are shaped and re-shaped continuously by the forces of nature, especially during winter months. Nothing ever seems to be the same twice. Heruclitus, the Greek philosopher said, "You can never step twice into the same river." That wisdom works here: You can never step twice onto the same beach. Tides, wind, rain and forces of nature wrestle with each other to dominate the scene. Landscapes are forever being altered. They are beautifully patterned textures formed by the energy, force and changing directions of the waves.

▲ *Some coastal community economics are devoted to having fun such as creating short lived sand sculptures.*

▲ *Proposal Rock is a popular place at springtime.*

The most dangerous thing in the world is to try to leap a chasm in two jumps.

- Lloyd George

▲ *Chocolate Labrador retriever following his master at Beverly Beach*

Oregon Beach Agates

Agates abound on certain beaches of the Oregon Coast. Some of the finest agates found in the world are on these beaches. The supply of stone is never exhausted. Agate fields are replenished by the wash that exposes them during the winter storms. The months October through April are generally the best times to hunt agates. February can be an ideal month with warmth in the air that is almost like spring with lots of sun shining on a calm surf.

Most agates are translucent. When held to the sunlight, formations or striations can be seen running through the glaciated structure of the stone. Opaque agates known as Jaspers have a crypto-crystalline variety of quartz running through the core in reds and browns. Jaspers are judged by these colors. Hunting for agates is more productive on the outgoing tides. If you walk facing the sun, they will be more apparent by their sparkle.

▲ *Polished agates glisten on the dunes*

Oregon Coast Agate Hunting Areas

- Nehalem Bay State Park

- Rockaway Beach

- Oceanside Beach Three Capes Loop

- Agate Beach State Recreation Site

- Moolack Beach

- Yaquina Bay State Recreation Site

- Neptune State Scenic Viewpoint

- Paradise Point State Recreation Site Port Orford

We can't own the sand. Sand slips through our outstretched hands. Beaches belong to the birds, to the shells, to the surf and to the tides. The beach belongs to a wide universe. In Oregon, the beach will always be there for people to enjoy.

Coast
Character

Fame is vapor, popularity an accident; riches take wings.
Only one thing endures, and that is character.

- Horace Greeley

Oregon, the state that flies with her own wings.

Whether it's the saltwater taffy bubbling in one of Oregon's oldest coastline candy stores, or stacks of well-cut wood for keeping hearth and home warm, or crab shacks, oyster outlets, cheese creameries, kite stores, and even smoked salmon stands...the long coastal highway has one universal thread that runs through it: Peculiar personality with lots and lots of character. It's that special character that sets the Oregon Coast apart from any other place.

This long, 363-mile strip of asphalt highway takes travelers through some of the country's most magnificent and stunning scenery. It also takes us by some displays of the most individualistic and independent, free-minded entrepreneurial efforts that you can find anywhere in America. After all, this is one of the last frontiers of the continental United States. Character of this sort demonstrates the singularity that comes from living near the sea. Some pursue happiness, others create it.

This kind of thinking holds up well on the coast. The best recommendation we can make is - sit back, relax and enjoy the ride. This is a unique part of the world unlike any other. What you will find in character on the Oregon Coast is worth every mile of the trip.

▲ *Coast Guard Petty Officer keeping watch on Yaquina Bay.*

◄ *Daydreaming on the Columbia River at Astoria's waterfront.*

We don't see things as they are,
we see them as we are.

- Anaïs Nin

Curiosity can take you to places ambition could never dream of.

- Mari Messer

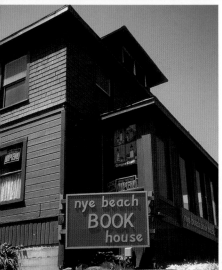

Glass

Centuries ago, when glass was first formed for utility as well as beauty, three essential elements for making glass were needed:

- Wood for its combustibility.

- Sand as the basic ingredient.

- Potash from ferns in the forest.

While all of these components are in ready abundance on the Oregon Coast, some techniques have changed.

Today, glass artists all along the coast rely on state-of-the-art kilns that control temperatures up to 2300 degrees with computers. Wood is no longer needed to fire the kiln. But, some of the other elements are still essential to glass blowing, including a willingness to blow through the pipe - breathing life into glass.

Glass can be made in almost any form – stained glass, slumped glass, glass mosaic, fused glass, beads, paperweights and other decorative pieces. Glassblowers are only limited by their imaginations. Several glass artists have created a hands-on format in their foundries.

A modern glass art renaissance underway all along the Oregon Coast from Astoria to Brookings. The coast is becoming known as one of the world's fastest growing regions for this ancient artform.

Visitors can use their creative imagination, under the artists' tutelage to create an individualistic work of art. It's a fun and warm way to spend a family afternoon together - especially if it happens to be raining.

Individuality of expression is the beginning and the end of all art.

- Goethe

Coast Churches

Here's the church and here's the steeple, open the doors and here are the people.

- From an old nursery rhyme

He that will learn to pray, let him go to sea.

- George Herbert

Having a place, a sanctuary that allows us to appeal to the heavens – a place to express our faith – is as fundamental as having a home. A dwelling to come back to.

Built by man, this place of worship is provided by the will, the patience and the blessings of an understanding God who knows the needs of people wishing to congregate for prayer and quiet reverence.

▲ *St. Mary The Virgin Episcopal Church, Gardiner, Oregon, "The Church with The Red Door."*

The first Episcopal services began in May 1877, when William Horsfall of Coos Bay, a pioneer Episcopal priest, traveled by horseback and buggy to hold services in the homes of the faithful along the Oregon Coast from Gold Beach to Florence.

St. Mary's is fondly referred to as "the church with the red door" and in 1990 was placed on the National Register of Historical Places.

Man makes holy what he believes, as he makes beautiful what he loves.

- Ernest Renan

▲ *St. John's Episcopal Church - Toledo, Oregon.*

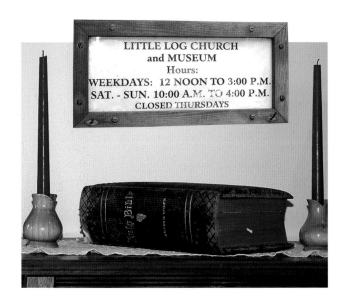

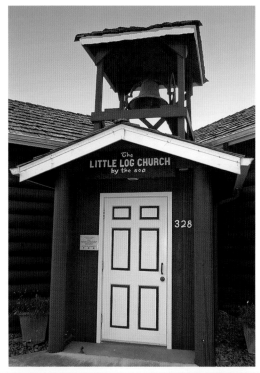

figure that God Almighty grew them trees and who am to charge anyone for some of them to build him a house.

straightforward statement ade by the logger who onated the logs used to build he Little Log Church in achats in 1929. This man ade no claims to religion.

▲ *Small sanctuary of The Little Log Church in Yachats, Oregon.*

Coast
Foods

So if you go for oysters, and I go for ersters,
I'll order oysters, and cancel the ersters,
Oysters, ersters. Ersters, oysters.
Let's call the whole thing off!

- Geroge & Ira Gershwin

Gi'e us Lord, a bit o' sun, a bit o' work, and a bit o' fun.
Gi'e us all, in the struggle and the sputter our daily bread and a bit o' butter.

- **An old Scottish grace**

Abundant is a word that percolates in our minds when we think about the native food stocks of the Oregon Coast. Old-timers remind us of the huge catches of the past decades, but we weren't here then. Most likely, you weren't either. So we concentrate on what is available today. We are pleased and gratified to live in a region that provides such delectable food delights. We savor the tastes that come from consuming unique flavors and textures.

At once, we think of wild Pacific salmon, succulent Dungeness crab, briny Oregon Coast oysters and lovely, wonderful melt-in-your-mouth coastal cheeses. Even though there are many more foods that are plentiful and readily available – all up and down Highway 101 - these are the items most favored by those who enjoy the flavors of the Oregon Coast.

When you get right down to it, it's your choice: You can fish for salmon and crab, gather your own oysters and make your own cheeses. Or, if that's not your thing to do, you can purchase these tasty items directly at the source, from fishermen and purveyors who will sell them to you at a cost that's hard to beat. Any way you want them, these foods are the culinary delights of the Oregon Coast.

Coast Foods

Cheese (chez) n. the curd of milk separated from the whey and prepared in many ways as a food.

Oys–ter (oi' star) n. any of several edible, marine, bivalve mollusks of the family *Ostreidae*, having an irregularly shaped shell, occurring on the bottom or adhering to rocks or other objects in shallow water.

Dun'ge –ness crab' (dun' ja nes') an edible crab, *cancer magister*, of shallow Pacific Coastal water from northern California to Alaska.

Salm–on (sam'an)n. a marine and fresh water food fish, *Salmo salar*, of the *Salmonidae*, having pink flesh, inhabitating waters off the North American coast near the mouths of large rivers, which it enters to spawn.

Say Cheese

When most Northwesterners think cheese, they think Tillamook.

Tillamook County is the county in Oregon best known for its dairy farming and the Tillamook County Creamery Association, the largest producer of cheese on the West Coast. So significant is this creamery that it alone stores 18 million two pound loaves in its product storage facility. Visualize this: if you were to place these loaves end-to-end, they would reach from Tillamook County to Chicago – some 1900 miles across the United States. With the beginning of the 21st century, records indicate that Tillamook County now exports 78 million pounds of cheese yearly. Additional markets are opening for distribution of this long-established and highly desired dairy product.

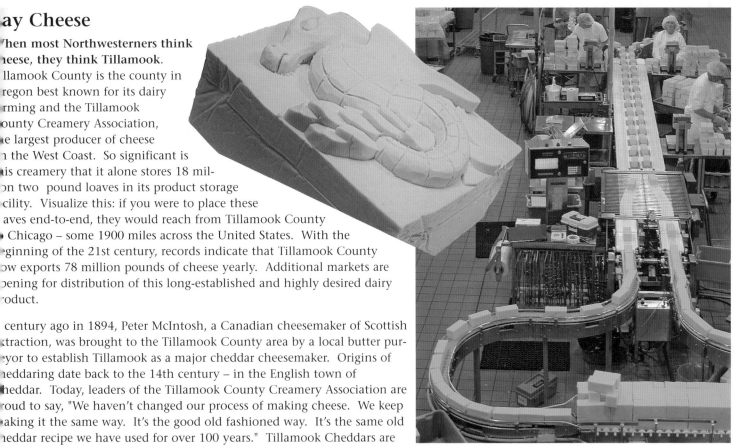

A century ago in 1894, Peter McIntosh, a Canadian cheesemaker of Scottish extraction, was brought to the Tillamook County area by a local butter purveyor to establish Tillamook as a major cheddar cheesemaker. Origins of cheddaring date back to the 14th century – in the English town of cheddar. Today, leaders of the Tillamook County Creamery Association are proud to say, "We haven't changed our process of making cheese. We keep making it the same way. It's the good old fashioned way. It's the same old cheddar recipe we have used for over 100 years." Tillamook Cheddars are desired and enjoyed by cheese connoisseurs throughout the world.

Happiness is that place between too little and too much Dungeness crab.

There's one thing 'bout oysters –

If you like'em, you can eat'em raw
right out of the shell –
right out of the bay –
cold and slurpy.

Shooters – is what they call 'em.
No tools needed to suck'em –
'cept you do need the knife to open'em.

And, you can cook'em.
Cook'em on the stove –
Cook'em in the oven –
Grill'em or stew'em –

There's dozens of ways to eat'em.
But, you do have to like'em.
That's the one thing 'bout oysters.

Overheard from an old oysterman

Coast Guard

Bless those who guard the shore
Bless those who come to the fore
Bless the waves and surf where spirits soar
Bless the boats and planes that carry them o'er.

"You have to go out -- you don't have to come back."

*- These are watchwords known to those who
serve in the United States Coast Guard.*

When merchant and pleasure boat sailors head into safe harbors, seeking shelter from nature's fiercest of gales, men and women of the United States Coast Guard – those crews who are willing to risk their lives in all kinds of weather – launch their crafts into rough waters.

Where dark lead gray skies and cold rain streams from low-lying clouds, black seawater throws off a creamy foam as it rolls up to shape the surf. These are daunting weather conditions for most experienced boatmen. But they are just some of the extreme conditions which routinely face Coast Guard personnel who train constantly to save lives, preserve waterborne property and protect the environment. As "Everyday Heroes" the Coast Guard are the primary guardians of America's waterways and coastlines. Even though the Coast Guard is the smallest of the U.S. Military Services, it is the largest and best trained of Coast Guards in the world.

The four main missions of the United States Coast Guard are National Security, Maritime Law Enforcement, Maritime Safety and Environmental Protection.

United States Coast Guard MLB Victory on morning patrol in Yaquina Bay.

▲ *Coast Guard Cutter at dockside inside of Astoria-Megler Bridge on the Columbia River*

Along the Oregon Coast, the Coast Guard serves from these stations...

- Ilwaco Station in Washington
- Garibaldi Lifeboat Station
- Yaquina Bay Station and Depoe Bay Station
- Siuslaw River Station
- Umpqua River Lifeboat Station
- Charleston Lifeboat Station
- Chetco River Lifeboat Station

▲ *Old Garibaldi Lifeboat Station*

The Northern Fortress

Coast Guard Stations at Yaquina Bay in Newport and in Depoe Bay, twelve miles north of Newport, are the northernmost units in Coast Guard Group North Bend. Both of these stations have the distinction of carrying the highest caseloads for search and rescue in the Thirteenth Coast Guard District. These caseloads average over three hundred a year. SAR (Search and Rescue) incidents include everything from disabled pleasure craft to commercial fishing boats extending to one hundred miles offshore.

Both Yaquina Bay and Depoe Bay Stations have responsibility for nearly sixty miles of coastline from the south of Cape Perpetua to the Haystack Rock twenty miles north of Depoe Bay.

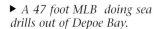

▲ *This 36 foot self-righting motor lifeboat is now de-commissioned and on display at Yaquina Bay Station.*

▶ *A 47 foot MLB doing sea drills out of Depoe Bay.*

"Typical day in the routine of the Coast Guard on the Oregon Coast"

Two fishermen aboard a sinking 33-foot salmon trawler were assisted by the Coast Guard near Yaquina Bay last week.

Gordon J. Tinsley, master of the Shelby Lynn, contacted the Coast Guard on VHF channel 16 at 8 p.m. on June 1 to report his vessel was disabled and taking on water.

Tinsley reported there was one foot of water in the bilge and the dewatering pumps were only operating on battery power and his engines were no longer operating because of flooding.

An HH-65 Dolphin helicopter from Coast Guard Group/Air Station North Bend and a 47-foot motor lifeboat and the 52-foot motor lifeboat Victory, both from Station Yaquina Bay, launched to assist. Coast Guard Group North Bend also issued an Urgent Marine Information Broadcast requesting assistance from mariners in the area.

At 12:30 a.m. on June 2, the Dolphin located the vessel in six-foot seas. The 47-foot motor lifeboat arrived minutes later and transferred a pump to the Shelby Lynn. The vessel was stabilized and safely towed by the Victory to Station Yaquina Bay.

As reported in The Siuslaw News 6/5/04

Do all the good you can,
By all the means you can,
In all the ways you can,
In all the places you can,
At all the times you can.

▶ *When conditions are at their worst, the Coast Guard is at its best!*

Victory "A State of Having Triumphed"

This steel-hulled 52-foot motor lifeboat was designed for off-shore rescue and built to sustain the worst of sea conditions. A self-righting and self-bailing craft of this design is manned by a crew of four and can carry up to 40 survivors.

Built in 1956, the *Victory* was designed and built in the Coast Guard Yard at Curtis Bay, Maryland. Having a cruising range of over 1000 miles, it was designed to replace the 52-foot wood-hulled motor lifeboats and to complement the shorter-legged 36-foot and 44-foot motor lifeboats. Being constructed entirely of steel adds range and endurance. Having a complete galley adds to the convenience of being at sea. In addition, the *Victory* is equipped with a 250-gallon per-minute pump for de-watering and fire fighting.

Victory and her sister ships, *Intrepid*, *Invincible II* and *Triumph II*, are the only four 52 foot MLBs in service today. They are stationed along the Oregon and Washington Coasts, which are considered the most challenging of coastlines on the continental United States. These are the only Coast Guard vessels under 65 feet in length with names.

In addition to the missions of search and rescue, the four vessels are assigned to fulfill missions of maritime law enforcement, marine environmental protection and recreational boating safety.

Because of the seaworthiness, durability and dependability of these four MLBs, it was recently decided by the Coast Guard to re-fit each of them with new power plants that will add range and some additional speed. New life has been given to each of these venerable craft.

Semper Paratus - Always Ready

Victory, 1956 CG-52312 U.S. Coast Guard Motor Lifeboat
Photos Courtesy of USGC

Don McMichael served as the last Executive Officer at Port Orford Lifeboat Station, which was in operation from 1934 until its closing in 1970. Before retiring from the United States Coast Guard in 1977, Don devoted his days to saving lives on one of the most dangerous coastlines in America – the Oregon Coast.

Following his career as a lifesaver, Don turned to his concerns for the pollution of oceans and the diminishing existence of marine mammals. "When I was young, the oceans were clean and abundant with life. But now our sea life has decreased and our oceans are endangered." Today, he communicates these concerns as one of the world's most acclaimed artists of marine mammal life. He translates his conservation interests onto canvas in his studio that overlooks Coos Bay. Don's Coast Guard career provided him an infinite knowledge of the sea, and he works in this second career to bring about awareness of how we can improve the future for our marine mammal life.

"We went out of here – Mac and me – and another guy – I don't remember his name, now...but, we took the call which was 50 miles right straight off of Blanco – it was dark and in the middle of winter. We were getting the crap kicked out of us by the waves and we spent the night out there. There's no place to sleep on those things. We didn't have wet suits in those days – or survival suits. And, there's always a certain amount of water in the bilges – no matter how often you pump it out of a wood boat. The only place you could lay down – that was anywhere near warmth was on the engine room deck grating. So, then you're getting bilge water slopped on you. Of course, you could sleep on the batteries but that wasn't a good idea either because you'd get battery acid on your clothes and your clothes wouldn't last long.

We left that rescue point later that afternoon and were in Coos Bay the next morning with the disabled boat in tow. It was a long, cold night."

Wayne Gage
Recollections from days
as a Coast Guardsman.

Wayne Gage, Commanding Officer at Port Orford Lifeboat Station served with Don McMichael as one of the last two to command this station before it was closed in 1970. Following that tour of duty, Wayne as Senior Chief Petty Officer was cited for heroism on the morning of December 27th, 1970 as Officer–in-Charge at the U.S. Coast Guard-Siuslaw River Station. Wayne engaged in the perilous rescue of three crewmen from the grounded fishing vessel, *Harold J.* The rescue took place south of Heceta Head Light Station.

The citation for the Coast Guard Medal commended him for entering the surf and swimming to the disabled vessel. In the heavy breaking surf, Wayne Gage demonstrated remarkable initiative, exceptional fortitude and daring in spite of imminent personal danger. He saved the lives of three men by making three separate trips swimming through the high surf. This act of heroism and unwavering devotion to duty as a lifesaver reflects the highest credit upon himself and the United States Coast Guard.

Even though Wayne has been retired from the Coast Guard for many years, he is still a man of the sea living upriver from Florence on the Siuslaw River in Mapleton – staying actively involved with boats.

"We'd go out under any conditions – it didn't matter what the weather was like – if somebody was drowning out there – we'd go out to try and save them."

Don McMichael
Recollections from days
as a Coast Guardsman

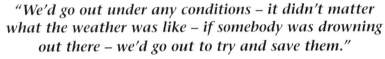

U.S. Coast Guard 36' MLB 36498 served as the motor lifeboat at the Port Orford Lifeboat Station until the station closed in 1970. Now this lifeboat is being carefully restored at Port Orford Heads State Park as part of the ongoing museum project which honors the surfmen who served in this most unusual

rescue station on the West Coast. Station crew members had to carry 5 gallon jerry cans full of fuel down 532 steps into Nellies Cove where the boat was launched out of the boathouse on rails into the surf … no matter how bad the conditions.

Coast Lighthouses

*Far in the bosom of the deep
O'er these wild shelves my watch I keep
A ruddy gem of changeful light.
Bound on the dusky brow of night.*

- Sir Walter Scott

In fact, all of these waters are dangerous. That is why, nowadays, almost anywhere Northwesterners can smell salt water, they can see the flash of navigational lights.

- **Legendary Lighthouses**
  John Grant and Ray Jones

you need a reason or…an excuse…to travel the **length of the Oregon Coast,** visiting lighthouses might just be your "ticket to de," on Highway 101.

ople from the world over seek out these sentinels of the shore that historically have protected seagoing craft from coastal disaster. owse any respectable bookstore, art shop or tourism center near a seacoast and you are certain to find plenty of information on ghthouses.

ong Oregon's 363 miles of magnificent coastline are nine lighthouses. At the northernmost point of the Oregon Coast is Tillamook ck Lighthouse standing 133 feet above the sea that completely surrounds it. This 62-foot tower, which was built on a basalt rock et, is now a columbarium, serving as a storage place for ashes of the deceased. Known as Terrible Tilly, it is and always has been a rribly difficult place to gain access.

rther down the coast is Cape Blanco Lighthouse, just above Brookings. This and all of the Oregon lighthouses, with the exception Terrible Tilly, are accessible for viewing and tours. One of the unique features of the Oregon Coast is its accessibility.

addition to the nine lighthouses that are included as part of the Oregon Coast Lighthouse grouping are two privately maintained ghthouses – *Cleft of The Rock Lighthouse*, which is a short distance south of Yachats, and *Pelican Bay Lighthouse* which serves as a light the Port of Brookings Harbor and Pelican Bay. The U.S. Coast Guard, Oregon State Parks Commission, Bureau of Land anagement and local volunteers, along with the spirit and energies of dedicated individuals of the Oregon Chapter of the U.S. ghthouse Society, keep the lights on, the structures white and the doors open to visitors.

◄ *Yaquina Bay Lighthouse in Newport was built in 1871. With its classic Cape Cod architecture, this wooden structure was restored in 1996 and serves as a popular museum and park. Yaquina Bay Lighthouse is Newport's oldest building and the second oldest lighthouse on the Oregon Coast.*

▲ *Heceta Head Lighthouse*

Heceta Head Lighthouse sits solidly on the precipitous 1000 foot high headland that is positioned midway between the north and south coasts of Oregon... a coast light to divide the dark space between Cape Arago and Cape Foulweather.

Don Bruno de Hezeta, the Portuguese explorer and navigator serving Spain in her explorations of the Pacific Northwest, is the source for the name Heceta Head. Considered the strongest light on the Oregon Coast, Heceta Head Lighthouse is now fully automated and the beacon is seen 21 miles from land. Heceta House, which was built in 1893 to accommodate the lighthouse keepers, functions today as a bed and breakfast inn.

Yaquina Head Lighthouse in Newport is the tallest of the lighthouses on the Oregon Coast. Standing at 93 feet on a headland reaching out into the Pacific Ocean it is 162 feet above sea level. Serving navigation entering Yaquina Bay, it was built in 1872. A complete restoration in 2006 will return the original colors; white on the 93-foot tower, black on the roof and gray trim.

Building the lighthouse

Yaquina Head's remote location was a challenge to building contractors in the early 1870s.

Wind, weather and loneliness tested the construction crews.

Twice, storms destroyed the small boats bringing freight to the site, and workers endured severe winter winds to frame the first dwellings.

▲ *Yaquina Head Lighthouse beacon has a classical first-order Fresnel lens. It flashes its light up to 19 miles away.*

Cleft of The Rock Lighthouse

Positioned on Cape Perpetua, the steepest rise of land directly above sea level on the Oregon Coast, this privately owned and functioning lighthouse was built in the early 1970's and put into service in 1979. The hymn "He Hideth My Soul In The Cleft of the Rock" is the source for this lighthouse's unusual name.

Tillamook Rock Lighthouse

Affectionately referred to as "Terrible Tilly" by the lighthouse keepers who had to withstand and survive terrible storms and high seas. Now, privately owned and functioning as a columbarium, "Terrible Tilly" provides a final resting place for the ashes of the deceased. For those whose remains lie here, the fiercest of storms have passed.

Cape Arago Lighthouse

Sitting on an islet just beyond Gregory Point this 44 foot tower has a light that was first illuminated in 1934. This is the third lighthouse to be built on this location. The two previous lights were destroyed by erosion from the ever persistent seas. Not open to the public; however, on some days you can get close enough to hear its unique fog horn.

outh of Reedsport are three historical lighthouses: Umpqua River, Coquille River and Cape Blanco lighthouses. These oastal beacons still stand as sentinels of the shore.

mpqua River Lighthouse was the first to be built on the Oregon Coast. It fell into the river due to shifting sands and had to be built in 1894. Standing at 165 feet above sea level, the tower emits a distinctive red and white flash over the sand dunes.

oquille River Lighthouse is two miles north of Bandon and is sometimes referred to as the Bandon Lighthouse. Sitting short nd squat alongside the Coquille River, its light guides mariners across a dangerous bar. It was first placed into service in 1896.

ape Blanco Lighthouse is the oldest continuously operating lighthouse on the Oregon Coast. At the westernmost point in regon, its light shines from a headland that is 245 feet above the ocean. Add 59 feet for the height of the tower and this light is onsidered one of the most prominent on the Oregon Coast.

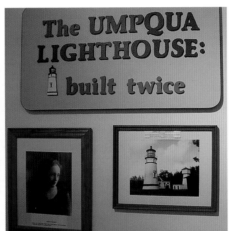

▲ *Cape Blanco Lighthouse*

Umpqua River Lighthouse   ▲ *Coquille River Lighthouse*

Coast
Museums

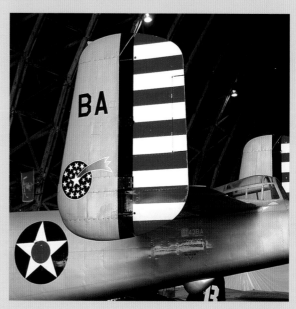

In the West the past is very close. In many places, it still believes it's the present.

- John Masters

Tomorrow hopes we have learned something from yesterday.

- John Wayne

The Oregon Coast isn't really steeped in history like other coastal communities on the North American continent. Some travelers might be surprised to learn that the museums and monuments on the coast were put in place mostly after the Civil War – unlike the eastern seaboard of America, where a substantial number of monuments were erected in declaration of America's independence from the British in 1776. But, all of these revolutionary goings-on necessarily preceded the opening of the Northwest. In fact, it helped to foster the eventual exploration of the Oregon Coast. Americans wanted more – from East to West.

And to the West they came... and are still coming! Initially, Thomas Jefferson, America's third president, believed America would acquire lands to be known as The Oregon Country – similar to the Louisiana Purchase. This land mass is known today as the states of Montana, Idaho, Oregon, Washington and the Canadian Province of British Columbia. In 1848, in an agreement with Great Britain, America ceded its rights to British Columbia and the Oregon Territory was formed. Later, in 1859, Oregon joined the union as the thirty-third state.

Sources for the name Oregon are unclear. Some scholars attribute the origins to Native Americans who coined the words *Ouragan* or *Origan,* believing these names were sourced from the great and mighty Columbia River. Other history buffs suspect the French, having just arrived from Wisconsin, made up their own version – *Ouisconsin.*

This and other facts and fancies from the past are what keep us frequenting the museums and monuments. Sourcing names is updated from time to time.

We like to paraphrase Arthur Campton who said, "Life in this twenty-first century undeniably has...such richness, joy and adventure as were unknown to our ancestors except in their dreams."

We hope you enjoy the museums and monuments as a testimony to the "good old days" - where history is still being made - today and tomorrow.

Astoria Column stands tall atop Coxcomb Hill overlooking Astoria - Oregon's oldest city on the coast. This monument originally dedicated in 1926, has been recently brought back to brightness to celebrate the bi-centennial of the journey of the Corps of Discovery.

▲ Fort Clatsop prior to the fire of 2005.

◀ A canoe named Okulam… meaning "sound of the ocean" was recently carved from a single old growth western red cedar log. The method used was from traditions passed on by the Chinook Nation.

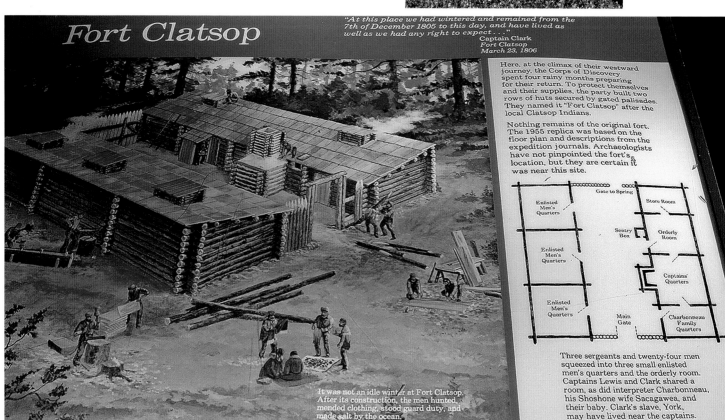

Fort Clatsop

"At this place we had wintered and remained from the 7th of December 1805 to this day, and have lived as well as we had any right to expect…"

Captain Clark
Fort Clatsop
March 23, 1806

Here, at the climax of their westward journey, the Corps of Discovery spent four rainy months preparing for their return. To protect themselves and their supplies, the party built two rows of huts secured by gated palisades. They named it "Fort Clatsop" after the local Clatsop Indians.

Nothing remains of the original fort. The 1955 replica was based on the floor plan and descriptions from the expedition journals. Archaeologists have not pinpointed the fort's location, but they are certain it was near this site.

Three sergeants and twenty-four men squeezed into three small enlisted men's quarters and the orderly room. Captains Lewis and Clark shared a room, as did interpreter Charbonneau, his Shoshone wife Sacagawea, and their baby. Clark's slave, York, may have lived near the captains.

It was not an idle winter at Fort Clatsop. After its construction, the men hunted, mended clothing, stood guard duty, and made salt by the ocean.

▲ Fort Clatsop, where Lewis and Clark spent the winter of 1805-1806 with The Corps of Discovery.

Tillamook Air Museum plays host to a variety of aviation's historic aircraft. A magnificently restored Consolidated-Vultee BT-13 used in World War II for flight instruction and reconnaissance circles in a bright blue sky preparing for a smooth landing.

Columbia River Maritime Museum provides space for a simulated Coast Guard rescue on the Columbia River Bar.

Today, the Columbia River Maritime Museum is considered one of the most interesting maritime museums on the West coast, this wide-windowed facility sits at water's edge on the Columbia River. It provides a living backdrop for historic fishing vessels and descriptions of the lives of Bar Pilots who undertake their dangerous missions of guiding ships over the treacherous bar at the mouth of Columbia River.

Oregon Coast Aquarium brings spectators face-to-face with some of the more mystical denizens of the deep. Green Anemones, Leafy Sea Dragons and skates share space in the aquarium with sharks, California sea lions , tufted puffins and pigeon guillemots. They all frolic in their own environment throughout Oregon's largest aquarium.

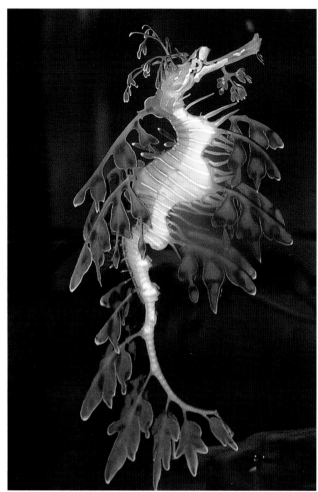

▲ *Green Anemone at the Oregon Coast Aquarium.*

▲ *Leafy Sea Dragons from the Great Barrier Reef in Australia. Few people get to see the Leafy Sea Dragon in their own natural habitat where only accomplished expert divers explore. A rarity in the Western States, they swim easily and carefree without fear of intrusion in a tall cylindrical tank positioned in the aquarium.*

▲ *Closeup of a skate at Oregon Coast Aquarium.*

Along the Oregon Coast, there are monuments commemorating our heritage as a free nation with a free spirit. Not always easy to find - these monuments are worth the seeking because they speak to the honor we feel as Americans always in search of our values that go with being free.

The Lincoln Statue in Lincoln City

Free-form bronze monument dedicated to the memory of Jesse M. Honeyman in the Jesse M. Honeyman Memorial State Park south of Florence.

"NO WORK IS MORE IMPORTANT THAN TEACHING THE CHILDREN THAT THE GOD-GIVEN BEAUTY OF OREGON IS THEIR HERITAGE."

Jesse Millar Honeyman
1852 -1948

"To the people of Lincoln City …as sharers in the noble history of the Old Oregon Territory, of which, in 1849, Abraham Lincoln was asked to be governor. The statue of Lincoln on horseback, reading, which I have this day given … is herewith commended to your special interest and concern. I hope that for you and your children, and for all who come after you in your beautiful State, it may stand as reminder of your own heritage and an inspiration not only to seek education in youth, but in the spirit of Lincoln, to find, in frustration and disappointed at any age, new opportunity through further education. With congratulations to the people of Lincoln City for what they have made of their own share of the great Oregon Territory, and the hope that your future may be glorious as your past was heroic."

Anna Hyatt Huntington
New York Sculptress

In her letter, dedicating her work of art, to the people of Lincoln City.

▲ *The statue of Abraham Lincoln currently stands on NE 22nd St., facing west, as part of the Lincoln City Community Center complex.*

Coast
Nature

Nature never did betray the heart that loved her.

- William Wordsworth

> *Nature is often hidden;*
> *sometimes overcome;*
> *seldom extinguished.*
>
> - Sir Francis Bacon

's an appropriate use of the word...colossal...when attempting to describe the wild abundance
flora and fauna that thrives on the Oregon Coast. A 50 mile wide, nearly 400 mile long eco-
stem is washed by the beneficial effects of the mighty Pacific Ocean. Innumerable species and
b-species of plants, trees, mammals, wildfowl, reptiles and amphibians are born, live and die in
is temperate ecosystem. In fact, there are so many that it would take a full-fledged encyclopedia
catalog the variety.

we explore the habitat and continue to seek what exemplifies the spirit of this environment, we
come more aware that a lifetime could be devoted to photographing nature's community that
rives in these coastal forests, rivers, estuaries, bays, intertidal zones, dunes, beaches, surf and
ean. It's immense. The word colossal seems just right.

Wildflowers thrive on this headland at Yaquina Head Outstanding Natural Area.

Yaquina Head Outstanding Natural Area, part of the Oregon Islands National Wildlife Refuge system which includes 1,853 rocks, reefs, and islands spanning 320 miles of the Oregon coastline provides safe sanctuary for harbor seals for breeding and haul-out sites. Here, harbor seal pups swim and cavort under the watchful eyes of the mama. In addition, more than thirteen species of seabirds including Brandt's cormorant, tufted puffin, and rhinoceros auklet and even the American bald eagle are protected from intrusion by the public.

An abundance of life
is on the move.
Sea lanes are the superhighway
of marine mammal traffic.
Plankton fuels the trip.

Coastal Birds

bald eagle
Haliaeetus leucocephalus

black oystercatcher
Haematopus bachmani

Brandt's cormorant
Phalacrocorax penicillatus

Cassin's auklet
Ptychoramphus aleuticus

common loon
Gavia immer

common murre
Uria aalge

double-crested cormorant
Phalacrocorax auritus

fork-tailed storm petrel
Oceanodroma furcata

glaucus-winged gull
Laurus hyperboreus

great egret
Ardea alba

Leach's storm petrel
Oceanodroma leucorboa

pelagic cormorant
Phalacrocorax pelagicus

pigeon guillemot
Cepphus columba

rhinoceros auklet
Cerorhinca monocerata

tufted puffin
Lunda cirrhata

western gull
Laurus occidentalis

white-crowned sparrow
Zonotrichia lencophrys

Bald Eagle An immature bald eagle *haliaeetus leucocephalus*, seeks a morning meal while soaring above the Yaquina Head Outstanding Natural Area. This magnificent resource has been maintained by the Bureau of Land Management since Congress established protection for this area in 1980. Slowly but surely, with restoration of salmon stocks and reduced harassment of nesting and feeding sites, the bald eagle is returning to its once notable position of pre-eminence among the majestic birds of prey.

▲ **Brandt's cormorant** *Phalacrocorax penicillatus*
Safely scattered in the surf zone up next to Yaquina Head, these nesting sea birds sit out their role of breeding on nests of sticks and seaweed. Having a peaceful sunny day to do it is a spring-time bonus.

And The Bogs Bloom, Too

Lysichiton americanum is a bright yellow plant found in marshes and bogs just inland from the surf. Discovered in America and blooming from early spring into June, it brings a brightness that catches the eye but not the nose. This plant is not named skunk cabbage without reason. A distinct and recognizable odor emanates from the stems and leaves as the plant ages. Another more attractive common name is used – swamp lantern - but the name skunk cabbage is how most of us know it. Beautiful or not, the smell of the skunk is real.

Finding beauty in a bog takes only eyes that seek beauty and a heart that revels in having found it.

▲ *Rare California cobra lilies* darlingtonia californica *flourish in this small swampy area near Mercer Lake in Florence.*

▲ *Skunk cabbage on the lower Salmon River.*

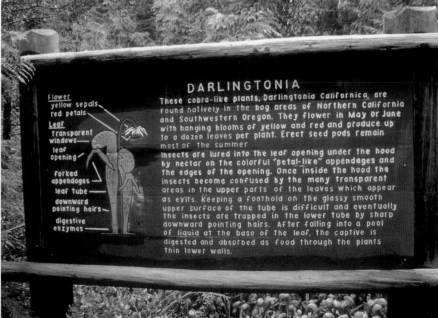

DARLINGTONIA

These cobra-like plants, Darlingtonia Californica, are found natively in the bog areas of Northern California and Southwestern Oregon. They flower in May or June with hanging blooms of yellow and red and produce up to a dozen leaves per plant. Erect seed pods remain most of the summer

Insects are lured into the leaf opening under the hood by nectar on the colorful "petal-like" appendages and the edges of the opening. Once inside the hood the insects become confused by the many transparent areas in the upper parts of the leaves which appear as exits. Keeping a foothold on the glassy smooth upper surface of the tube is difficult and eventually the insects are trapped in the lower tube by sharp downward pointing hairs. After falling into a pool of liquid at the base of the leaf, the captive is digested and absorbed as food through the plants thin lower walls.

flower
yellow sepals
red petals
Leaf
transparent windows
leaf opening
forked appendages
leaf tube
downward pointing hairs
digestive enzymes

*t is not the language of
he painter but the lan-
uage of nature to which
ne has to listen.*

- Vincent van Gogh

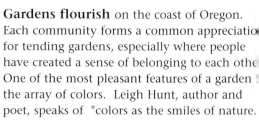

Gardens flourish on the coast of Oregon. Each community forms a common appreciatio[n] for tending gardens, especially where people have created a sense of belonging to each othe[r]. One of the most pleasant features of a garden [is] the array of colors. Leigh Hunt, author and poet, speaks of "colors as the smiles of nature.[”]

▲ *Shore Acres State Park on the Cape Arago Highway*

Some people are always grumbling because roses have thorns. I am thankful that thorns have roses.

- Alphonse Karr

hat buzzing-noise means something. You don't get a buzzing-noise like at, just buzzing and buzzing, without its meaning something. If there's buzzing noise, somebody's making a buzzing-noise, and the only reason r making a buzzing-noise that I know of is because you're a bee. nd the only reason for being a bee that I know of is making honey. nd the only reason for making honey is so as I can eat it. at then again, you never can tell with bees.

- Winnie-The-Pooh, A.A. Milne

▲ *White-Crowned Sparrow.*

That buzzing noise means something.

How much finer things are in composition than alone.

- Ralph Waldo Emerson

He who plants a garden, plants happiness.

- Chinese proverb

Shore Acres is a garden for all seasons.

Common Loon

Common Loons, *gavia immer*, lie lower in the water due to their solid bone structure. Well adapted to their diving lifestyle, their bodies resemble a miniature nuclear-powered submarine. They cruise about seeking tasty tidbits like tiny crabs. Loons dive to depths of 180 feet in search of their meal.

Usually, the loon (a word derived from the Scandinavian Lom meaning clumsy) can be spotted on the open ocean close to shore and in estuaries and freshwater lakes. The loon's voice is unmistakable: a long wailing note not unlike the sound of a complex yodel. Often it is referred to as loon laughter.

◄ *The Common Loon, no known to nest in Oregon, finds its food on open ba and freshwater lakes. The two showed up unexpecte in Coos Bay.*

Great Egret

Great egrets *Ardea alba* hunt their prey with fixed concentration. With keen eyes, this white feathered, elegant bird stands patiently in marshy water filled areas. It watches and waits for the slightest movement. Suddenly, this great egret will pluck its prey from the shallow water. Dinner is served!

◄ *Found on the southern Oregon Coast in lower rivers and estuaries, the great egret stands and waits for its food.*

Dean Creek Elk Viewing Area

East of Reedsport lies a spectacular 1,095-acre wildlife refuge that provides a safe haven for nearly 100 Roosevelt elk, giving these majestic animals a place to rest, breed and feed without fear of harm.

In a land exchange nearly twenty years ago, the Bureau of Land Management acquired the property. Now, working with the Oregon Department of Fish and Wildlife, the BLM manages this substantial parcel of protected land. They provide a sheltered viewing platform, interpretive displays and interactive panels explaining the habitat and the vagaries of the refuge inhabitants.

▲ *Black tailed deer are common to the Coast Range and will forage in the marshy areas close to the ocean.*

◄ *Roosevelt elk rest at noon but stay alert and on the watch for intruders.*

◄ *Early in the day, elk feed on the grasses that are abundant in this temperate climate.*

The O.H. Hinsdale Interpretive Center an enjoyable experience allowing the spectator a comfortable viewing station to watch migrating Canada geese along with numerous other waterfowl.

Bald eagles, great blue herons, Osprey and many songbirds share this land wi black tailed deer, beaver, nutria, muskr and an occasional visitor – the black be

Whale Watching On The Oregon Coast

"Whale Watch Spoken Here" signs dot the Oregon Coast. Southern migration begins in December. The peak time for sighting whales is in the first week of January. Pods containing as many as thirty whales an hour can pass the coast on any given day.

Gray whales are the common mammal found in this long round-trip journey of 10,000 miles or more. This time of year, gray whales migrate from their summer feeding grounds in the Bering Sea and the Chuckchi Sea north of Alaska. When they pass the Oregon Coast, they are eager to reach their breeding and calving areas in the warmer waters of the lagoons of Baja California … Mexico's frontier territory.

Winter migrants stay off the coast by as much as two miles. Good binoculars are a practical piece of equipment for spotting whales. Scan the area between the points of jetties and look halfway to the horizon.

In the spring migration, the whales, with their newborns, stay closer to the coast and are often easier to see. Just look beyond the surf-line and into the mouths of rivers flowing to the ocean. Sometimes, gray whales will swim between jetties…just as this one did.

Gray whales, traveling north in the spring, travel in small family groups of about four mammals. Good opportunities for spotting them up-close are at the mouth of the Chetco River, from the jetty at Coquille River and along Cape Ferrelo.

Whale Watching From The Beach

Catch sight of the whales as they pass by the Oregon Coast on their annual migrations. Many of these viewing platforms with binoculars are available along the migration route.

Coast
Patterns

Patterns, textures and reflections are suddenly there – especially when you least expect them. Abstract impressions are subtle departures from the realism of the moment.

It's common to overlook what is near, by keeping the eye fixed on something remote.

- Samuel Johnson

ture surprises us. So does light, color and unique arrangements of how one element plays off the other. Patterns form designs ating motifs that either please or offend the eye. But, the orderliness sets a method of repetition. This repetition either appeals to or it's lost on our visual observation. Patterns are everywhere on the coast... in the trees, the beaches, the surf, the shadows and the lections. Whether walking, riding or flying, we look constantly. And we're continuously rewarded.

xtures can be, at once, smooth or they can be coarse. The roughness is often random. Texture shows its beauty more in sand and ndstone structures. Characteristics that appeal to us are those that come as a result of the forces of nature; forces that come from f, salt and wind combining to create their own designs. Imagination steps in to help. The intermixture of patterns and textures let form, in our mind's eye, images that add a vitality to the experience. Mother Nature never disappoints us if we use a vivid imagina-n and take the time to view her beautifully created compositions.

pressions are a combination of what we see and what we think we see. We can depart from the realism of what we see and let agination take hold of what we want to do with what we see. We can metamorphose our objective intake into a subjective tapestry canvas of our own making. It's a creative release from reality. Sometimes it's more rewarding to blur the reality; thus, making the ult an expression of inner artistic perception rather than an absolute replica of an image. Creating an impression from a realistic servation needs only one's own approval and imagination.

Reflections are at once there, and then gone. Oftentimes, much too soon.

◄ *End of summer on Cleawox Lake at Jesse M. Honeyman Memorial State Park.*

77

Sandstone Sculptures

Always in search of nature's awesome handiwork and surprising artistic designs, we come upon the wonders of *tafoni* at Shore Acres State Park. *Tafoni* is the Italian word for naturally formed hollows and caverns etched in sandstone. The myriad of honey-combed labyrinths form lacey patterns of hollows, pits and ridges. They are caused by the constant action of tidal washes etching patterns into the sedimentary rock -- rock consisting of sand, quartz and silica, cemented by natural elements of calcium carbonate, iron oxide and clay.

Tafoni is formed by the waves washing up and over vertical and near-vertical sandstone surfaces. Because of their vertical stature, these surfaces are less affected by direct hits from waves. Erosion is gentle and gradual. The delicate washing process creates intricate patterns that take on the appearance of coarsely woven lace. Variations abound on the southern Oregon Coast. No two are alike, nor do they ever stay the same. Nature changes the patterns with each incoming and outgoing tide. Tidal variations provide a constantly changing palette.

he finest workers in stone are not copper or steel tools,
t the gentle touches of air and water working at their
isure with a liberal allowance of time.

- Henry David Thoreau

A man is a very small thing and the night is very large and full of wonders.

- Lord Dunsany

A good eye makes us see. What we see lies there before us. It only takes imagination to spark our awareness of what surrounds us. Magic is everywhere. When we find patterns, textures and reflections that enhance our experience, visualization becomes the reality that feeds our souls and our hearts.

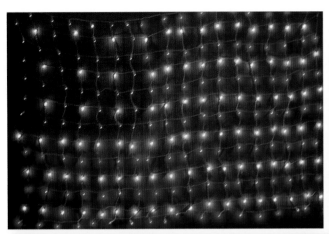

◄ *A patriotic display of lights following the tragic attack on the Twin Towers on September 11th, 2001.*

▲ *Lighted stairs lead to the beach in Lincoln City. Accommodations for access to the beach are found all along the Oregon Coast.*

◄ *Oncoming late evening traffic casts a glow over the Siuslaw River Bridge.*

The question is not what you look at but what you see.

- Henry David Thoreau

◄ *Looking across the Siuslaw River under the Siuslaw River Bridge in Florence.*

Coast
Rivers

All rivers flow into the sea,
yet the sea is never full;
To the place from which they flow,
the rivers flow back again.

- Ecclesiastes 1:7

Time is a flowing river. Happy those who allow themselves to be carried, unresisting, with the current. They float through easy days. They live, unquestioning, in the moment.

- Christopher Morley
From *Where The Blue Begins*

vers, growing from high in the mountains, cascade down to the coast. Feeding forestland, irrigating coastal plains and flooding tuarial and rocky inter-tidal areas, these rivers of the West are an integral part of the Oregon Coast's ecosystem.

esh water flowing through these estuaries is rich in natural nutrients. Sea life and other enticing ingredients like phytoplanktons d zooplanktons flourish in these abundant bowls of plenty. The nourishing concoction lures salmon and steelhead on their inland urney to spawn – propagating new life in a cycle of one of nature's most grandiose schemes.

ative American names have been given to some of these wonderful western rivers, like Nehalem, Nestucca, Siletz, Siuslaw, Umpqua d the Yaquina Rivers.

en, there is the Great River of the West– the Columbia River. First charted in 1792 by Captain Robert Gray, when he sailed the merican ship **Columbia Rediviva**, this huge flowing river moves its volume of water through a deep gorge carved through mountains d empties to its mouth in the Pacific Ocean. Here, the great river earned its nickname, "Graveyard of the Pacific" because of the ldly variable currents and winds of up to sixty miles per hour. Over the years, many shipwrecks have occurred because of the acherous sandbars at the Columbia's mouth.

▲ *A sailboat regatta plays out under the watchful eye of the magnificent Mount Hood. The Columbia River is host to many activities, both trade and recreational. It is the major river in the Northwest that is Oregon's north border with Washington as it flows on its way to the Oregon Coast.*

▲ *Sternwheelers are still part of the economy on coast rivers. Today, pleasure and entertainment a more common than commercial use: Dinner cruises on the Siuslaw River provide local history of t Florence area.*

▲ *Drift Creek flows serenely into Siletz*

▲ *"Sometimes a Great Notion"...the film adaptation of Ken Kesey's first major literary success was filmed at this house on the Siletz River. Henry Fonda, Paul Newman and Lee Remick were major stars.*

Time is like a river made up of events that happen, and its current is strong; no sooner does anything appear than it is swept away, and another comes in its place, and will be swept away too.

- Marcus Aurelius

John Day River named after John Day of the Astor-Hunt overland party which preceeded the Lewis and Clark Corps of Discovery.

▲ *Nehalem River sweeps through pastureland past the town of Nehalem, an Indian name for "place where people live." The Coast Range is in the background.*

Sweet Creek Falls

Sweet Creek flows northward to empty into the Siuslaw River at Point Terrace just below the small town of Mapleton.

It only takes
a drop of water
to start a waterfall.

- Erin Brokovich

Coast Sand Dunes

Weather is always doing something there; always attending strictly to business; always getting up new designs and trying them on people to see how they will go.

- Mark Twain, 1876

Mother Nature has a way of fulfilling our fantasies: She can arrange sand, water, trees, sky and space; add birds and animals; and then put wildflowers and water lilies in such places that leave us in awe of the wonder of it all.

The clock that regulates the pace of most things in life and the same timepiece that helps create a cadence for nature seems to allow for a slower meter on the sand dunes of the Oregon Coast. Sand shifted by the wind doesn't respond with much urgency here, even when high-volume winds go to work on the surface.

In the nearly 7000 years that the Oregon Dunes have been slowly and methodically building their own phenomena, there have been no fast-paced changes. But, over the years, physical changes have taken place; new shapes have formed, patterns have changed and the overall topography has been designed and re-designed. It's difficult to discern the changes. When sand and water are mixed together by the wind, nothing stays either constant or permanent. The only constant in the equation of this natural phenomenon is the growing volume of sand granules that are naturally formed by nature at work.

Considered to be the largest coastal sand dunes in North America, this area is designated as the Oregon Dunes National Recreation Area. Overseen by the U.S. Forest Service, it is part of the Siuslaw National Forest. This strip of wonderful natural resource extends south of Florence on the south side of the Siuslaw River almost to the Coos Bay region. The dunes are piled onto what is known as the Coos Bay Dune Sheet which is a gently sloping terrace of solid marine sandstone. Comprised of 32,186 acres of spectacular sand dunes, streams, lakes, marshes and forests, its length is forty-plus miles - all along the coastline of the Pacific Ocean.

Dunes reaching 500 feet above sea level dominate the scenery. The sand with fjord-like fingers, extends inland to the Coast Range Mountains – in some places as far as three miles. These dunes are like no other in the world. Some of the formations take on proportions reminiscent of the Sahara Desert. They rise like buttes above the valleys and swales that have been washed out by waves and wind. Other dunes have parabolic designs forced by the whims of wind-whipping winter rain storms – with gusts sometimes up to 100 miles per hour. High oblique ridges constitute great masses that run inland from the ocean. They are so-called because their crests are aligned obliquely to the directions of both the summer and the winter winds. Some of these ridges are more than 6000 feet in length and stand hundreds of feet above sea level. Scientists believe they are the only kind on earth. On this 40 plus miles of coastline lies one of the world's geological wonders with a constantly – but slowly – changing geography. The domineering forces of nature have come together to provide an environment that invites hiking, fishing, canoeing, kayaking, horseback riding, camping, photography and all-terrain vehicle use. It's another one of those fantastic places on our Oregon Coast for adventure as well as spiritual renewal.

To see a world in a grain of sand,
and heaven in a wildflower,
hold infinity in the palm of your hand,
and eternity in an hour.

- William Blake

If there is magic on this planet it is contained in water.

- Loren Eisley

Water Lilies in the Sand Dunes

After the Ice Age, melting glaciers left chunks of ice behind. These huge chunks melted and eventually created potholes and depressions in the boggy areas of the sand dunes. As these sunken areas filled with water, natural ponds formed giving life to water lilies.

Wind, Water and Sand

Summer winds are soft. They blow steadily from the north and northwest at a leisurely 12-15 miles per hour. Coast Range Mountains and their lower hills act as buffers, deflecting wind currents. Sculpting of the dunes goes on continuously always forming new shapes.

Winter winds are usually even lighter than the steady summer winds. However, during severe winter storms, winter winds can exceed 100 miles per hour. Blowing from the south and southwest, winds move large amounts of sand reshaping dunes and altering the higher ridges of the oblique dunes.

Water plays a large part in the formation of these coastal dunes. Ocean currents, flowing from the south in the winter and the north in the summer, gather and hold sediment from rivers emptying at the ocean side. Sand is dredged from the ocean floor by the constantly shifting tides, currents and powerful waves. When the water does its job of dumping the sand on the beach it forms the first layer of dunes known as transverse dunes. Then, the wind takes over and deposits the sand in all kinds of natural formations. For some of us, it's like gazing at images of old world paintings with their alluring and soothing textures displaying abstract patterns and symmetrical shapes.

When you come to the fork in the road - take it.

- Yogi Berra

inding Tracks
the Sand

aking assessments of what might be
autiful and what is not leaves us want-
g and sometimes frustrated. It's almost
usory. You can find a line made from
e wind in the sand and relish its natural
auty. Or, you can spy a series of tracks
ade by man and his toys and still appre-
ate how light creates an artful form.

en though these lines are from different
rces there is a connection between the
o in spite of their lack of similar ori-
ns.   Each of these lines in the sand was
ade unpredictably. Their essence is a
sult of how the sand accepts the intru-
on on its ever evolving and depthless
irface.

Sea Stacks, Surf and Tidepools

The ocean throws itself against the coast,
creating unique forms of misshapen statuary;
piling waves in huge rolling cascades;
then, it gently washes its own sea urchins.
Is this not a place of immense grandeur?

e wonder what the first impression was for early explorers. Sir Francis Drake and later, the Spaniard Bartholome Ferrelo, spied ese weird looking mini–mountains mostly made of basalt, or hardened lava. The formations were created by eruptions coming from me groups of fissures that poured lava from the Columbia Plateau. Lava flowed from the lower end of the Columbia River. This hot, olten substance intruded in the soft marine sediments building layers as it cooled. Then, the layers building on previously cooled vers, solidified as igneous rock, each layer cooling on the past one. Gradually the basalt hardened and remained buried for eons. ajor headlands formed as land lifted. The softer and more fragile elements of soil and sand sediments sifted away. Ice Age erosion gan exposing large rock formations. Continuously washed by the ocean and rain and with lowering sea levels, these wondrous sea cks began to look like hay piled high in the fields after harvest. As this image became more prominent, it was easy for early settlers refer to the sea stacks as "haystack" rocks.

Cannon Beach stands Haystack Rock, a 235-foot monolith of basalt accompanied by lesser protrusions surrounding it. These are led Needles. Another haystack rock stands even taller at 327 feet. It is off of Cape Kiwanda. While taller than Cannon Beach's ystack Rock by nearly 100 feet, this monolith is seen by fewer people - only because Cannon Beach is a more popular tourist desti- tion. Smaller sea stacks and minor monoliths dot the coast of Oregon. All of these natural formations provide refuge for wildlife: eller's sea lions, cormorants, puffins, common and marbled murrelets...to name just a few of the wildlife inhabitants.

From this point I beheld the grandest and most pleasing prospect which my eyes ever surveyed.

- Captain William Clark
  January 1806

▲ *A soft winter sunset silhouettes the sea stacks at Pistol River.*

▲ *Sea stacks stand guard over the Harris Beach Marine Garden which is part of the Oregon Islands National Wildlife Refuge.*

▲ *Whaleshead Rock sits stationary in the water off-shore, even as whales pass by in their migrations up and down the coast.*

This monolithic sea stack stands tall on the beach at
pe Blanco.

▲ *Unusual rock and sea stack formations lie along the Oregon Coast.
Arch Rock provides a shaded refuge in its open and accessible arch to the sea.*

▲ *Cold winter air brings silvery light shining across the pewter-like gray of an incoming sea beneath Cascade Head.*

Moolack Creek empties to the Pacific Ocean. It was known to the Chinook Indians as a good place to hunt. Moolack was jargon for elk.

Winter storms on the coast have a peculiar effect on visitors. Rather than discouraging people from visiting, they draw people to the coast: Storms attract spectators because of their dynamic turbulence. Some storm watchers make an extra effort to be at the coast when the storms are at their worst. Or, as some would say it, when storms are at their best.

Storms are strong climatic forces caused by global patterns of air circulation. The local topography reacts to the forces powered by the sun that heats the earth's surface in uneven patterns. As moist air is drawn up along the Oregon Coast, some twelve feet of rain pours down creating a lushness along the coast and into the Coast Mountain Range. These productive forests hold back the gale force winds keeping storms from spilling over into valleys between the Coast Range and Cascades.

What are the effects of these winter storms? Sand dunes are formed and re-shaped to provide an ever changing land environment. Shorefront elevation is changed by the continuous redesign of capes, headlands and promontories. Vegetation along the coastline responds to whatever nature forces upon it. Old growth trees are blown down. They take on a new life as nurse logs to propagate fresh growth and to serve as wildlife nest sites, thereby benefiting the environment.

Stinging sea salt, driven by gale force winds, comes in many carriers – waves, breakers, sneaker waves and huge rollers that can reach heights of twenty feet. The storm-driven salt helps control vegetation on the shore and helps to re-shape the dunes. Sand, liberated the storm winds, creates parabola dunes and spreads sediment along the beaches.

Storm watching can be so entrancing and exhilarating that many visitors make it a destination during the winter months. They even have a habit of calling ahead to inquire about the weather forecast...hoping that an impending storm will hit the coast at a time to their plans.

▲ *Winter brings a new slant to the setting sun. As it slides toward the horizon, a softer, magical light washes the crashing surf at day's end in Boiler Bay.*

In Yachats, winter storms are likened to grand crescendos. Some residents in this musically – oriented community say "storms crash in here with the drums and cymbals of a John Philip Sousa march." While it is a colorful metaphor, the volumes of noise are similarly resounding.

▲ *A strong winter surf sweeps over Agate Beach.*

Surf's Up At Boiler Bay. We photograph the Oregon Coast at eye level. This is a conscious decision. We want to encourage other travelers to see the coast of Oregon from its many scenic viewpoints. We place our cameras in those areas that are accessible to all travelers. There is very little physical risk doing it this way.

Being a restless pair of photographers and always seeking what is beyond the next turn in the road keeps us energized. Being on the look-out for something to surprise us is what keeps us in the hunt, like sighting this board surfer who makes *merry* just before Christmas with a glorious day of surfing at Boiler Bay.

A symphony of the surf.
Mother Nature is the conductor.
The surfer is the featured soloist.

Tidepools and Tidal Washes

Tidepools along with the sea-washed sedimentary shore platforms of basalt are created and then renewed regular by the dynamics of changing tides and washing waves. It's an ever-evolving palette replenished by diverse creatures bringing their own pigments to this colorful canva painted by Mother Nature.

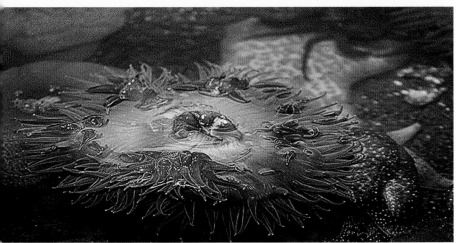

Teach us delight in simple things.
  - Rudyard Kipling

Sunup
and
Sundown

What the eye sees, the heart never forgets.

- Malawaian proverb-Malawi, Africa

*I have always been delighted at the prospect of a new day, a fresh try, one more start,
with perhaps a bit of magic waiting somewhere behind the morning.*

- J.B. Priestley

Suddenly darkness releases its hold on the night and a new day is born. With determination, the sun rises in the east, spreading light on land and water – bringing us another God-given day.

Later in the day, sunset slips beyond the horizon and the waves continue to force their way onto the beaches. Tides fall and rise again bringing a pulse of life. There is wonder in this place that arranges itself with such color and light.

Autumn brings a special glow to the sunrise at Yaquina Bay.

◄ *Peace and tranquility reflects from the evening sun at Oceanside, a tiny hamlet set on a steep slope just south of Cape Meares Lighthouse.*

Sun of The Ocean

*Good wishes to you
sun of the ocean
as you travel across the sky.*

*We follow your voyage
seeing how you fill the heavens
giving birth to the stars.*

*Into the ocean you slide.
Day comes to an end
leaving no hurt or harm.*

*Light reflects from your passage
rising now as the moon.
Will this be the promise of your return?*

　　　　　　　　　- Angus B. Campbell

Behold the bewitching hours.
Colors play on a canvas
of the natural world with
impressionistic rays of light.
Clouds become the sculptures
of the sky.

nter sunset at Beverly Beach.

Sundown at Seaside Beac

Night Music

When we hear the surf and its sound
we sense the flow, the force and the pound.
Waves over waves upon the shore sweep.
At peace, we slowly slide off to sleep.

Hushed notes linger in turns of tide and time.
The tunes are from the surf and its rhyme.
Night music sings to us from the shore,
with melodies lifting our spirits even more.

We are grateful for this slumber on our side.
Little do we care for the changes of tide.
Comfort comes from this natural power.
Our strength is being restored by the hour.

On the new morn with a stretch and a yawn,
we go out eager to greet the new dawn.
It's there we meet the prospects of another day.
Our wish is to bring cheer to those whom we may.

Sundown at Driftwood Shores.

Spirit of Place!

The more we travel the Oregon Coast, up and down and back again, the more we realize there are still places hidden away – yet to be found.

There are more sights, more vistas, more people, daily sunrises and some spectacular sunsets; more events, more boats, more wildlife, more gardens and wildflowers blooming on coastal banks. We revel in the unexpected surprises. These are the times we are grateful for Highway 101. It provides such convenient access to this magnificently beautiful coastline.

But, now we come to the end of this journey and we offer this following tribute to:

The Spirit of the Oregon Coast

How will we know you the next time?

Will you have carved out new pocket beaches?

Will you have shaved off new cliffs?

Will you have rearranged sea stacks in the surf?

Will more sand have shifted in the dunes?

Will you add more tidal washes and tidepools?

Will you form new shapes in the bays?

Will you enlarge the estuaries?

Will there be more museums and monuments to visit?

How about your patterns and textures? Will they have changed too?

Reflections are always shifting. We know they will be changed with new light and new shapes.

Sunrises and sunsets are your daily specialty. They are always different. Thank the heavens for their phenomena.

We'll go upriver when we can because we know how much the flow of fresh water means to the health and well-being of your estuaries.

And, then there are those classically designed bridges. We can only hope they will remain the same in architectural style and design.

We will watch where the Pacific Ocean batters up against towering sea cliffs.

We will see coastal forests drenched in fogs that penetrate deep into the tree line.

We don't know what you have in store for us on our next trip. And, we accept the notion that there will always be change because change is part of the bargain that is constant with life and the living of it. So until we meet again, we leave you with this thought:

It Takes Just One Grain of Sand

As we walk the vast open stretches of beach we will take the time to hold just one grain of sand to the sky and promise to care for this magnificent place. When we do this, we will have engaged in a process to conserve this treasure. It's a trust for future generations. What greater legacy can we pass along to those who follow us?

- Acknowledgements -

We thank those who have provided us assistance, advice and helpful hints as we have traveled the Oregon Coast. It's like being in a very friendly neighborhood – filled with spirited people who are willing to share their time and friendship.

Some of these people stand out in our minds and we wish to acknowledge their interest in this project. They have provided support, encouragement and contributions of knowledge to the formation of this book; so, in alphabetical order:

Jerry Flores, an active duty Coast Guardsman stationed at Yaquina Bay Station assisted us willingly and energetically compiling information. Jerry provided us photos of those magnificent motor lifeboats that are manned by men and women of the U.S. Coast Guard in their efforts to save lives and property on the Oregon Coast.

Wayne Gage and Don McMichael served at Port Orford Lifeboat Station. Wayne was its last Commanding Officer. Following his command here, Wayne served as Officer-in-Charge at the U.S. Coast Guard Siuslaw River Station. It was there that he engaged in the perilous rescue of three crewmen from a grounded fishing vessel. Senior Chief Petty Officer Gage entered the surf and swam to the disabled vessel making three separate trips to rescue the seamen. For this act of courage and unwavering devotion to duty, Wayne Gage was awarded the Coast Guard Medal which is awarded only to those who perform voluntary acts of heroism in the face of great personal danger.

Don McMichael gave us time and willing explanations of his experiences as a career Coast Guardsman on the Oregon Coast. His service as Executive Officer of Port Orford Lifeboat Station before it was decommissioned in 1970 is exemplary of a career that was filled with dedication to duty and a desire to save lives of people at risk in the sea.

 Judy Nedry, author, editor and teacher saw places where our syntax was committing sins. She set us on the straight and narrow path to better prose and poetry. We appreciate her efforts and counsel.

Rob O'Lenic has worked with us on a variety of print and graphic projects. What more can we say than he is a very patient professional and plays an important role in guiding our projects through to a polished finish.

Matthew St. Clair took us on a tour of the Yaquina Bay Station, which included a very instructional description of two life saving boats: The 52' Victory and a 47' Motor Lifeboat. His dedication to the Coast Guard is most impressive and his knowledge of the equipment used by the Coast Guard is a reassurance to all of us of the on-going excellence of our military and the part it plays in the protection of our nation.

Bibliography

Putting together any project that shares information is a task that is always made easier when sources of information are readily available. Here in Oregon, we are blessed with great repositories of compiled data. Bookstores thrive in this part of the world and an excellent library system exists in spite of many of the funding curtailments common in the economics of today. We have made use of the following sources of information and commend these to those who wish to travel and thrive in *The Spirit of The Oregon Coast*.

- **America's Western Edge**
  John M. Thompson ©2005
  Phil Schermeister, Photographer
  Publisher: National Geographic Society
  ISBN 0-7922-3811-7
  ISBN 0-7922-3812-5

- **Oregon Geographic Names**
  Lewis A. McArthur 1883-1951
  Sixth Edition Revised and Enlarged
  Lewis L. McArthur ©1992
  Publisher: Oregon Historical Society
  ISBN 0-87595-236-4

- **The Oregon Book - Information A to Z**
  Connie Hopkins Battaile ©1998
  Publisher: Connie Battaile
  ISBN 0-9657638-2-X

- **Fire at Eden's Gate**
  Tom McCall & The Oregon Story
  Brent Walth ©1994
  Publisher: Oregon Historical Society
  ISBN 0-87595-247-X

- **Pacific Destiny**
  The Three Century Journey
  to the Oregon Country
  Dale L. Walker ©2000
  Publisher: Forge Books
  ISBN 0-312-86933-9

- **Oregon Coastal Access Guide**
  Mile-by-Mile Guide to Scenic and
  Recreational Attractions
  Kenn Oberrecht ©2002
  Publisher: Oregon State University Press
  ISBN 0-87071-491-0

- **The Northwest Coast – A Natural History**
  Stewart T. Schultz ©1990
  Publisher: Timber Press
  ISBN 0-88192-142-4

- **Birds of Oregon**
  Roger Burrows & Jeff Gilligan ©2003
  Publisher: Lone Pine Publishing
  ISBN 1-55105-374-8

- **Exploring the Seashore**
  A Guide to Shorebirds and
  Intertidal Plants and Animals
  Gloria Snively ©1978
  Publisher: Gordon Soules Book Publishers Ltd.
  ISBN 0-919574-25-4

- **The Photographer's Guide to the Oregon Coast**
  David Middleton and Rod Barbee ©2004
  Publisher: The Countryman Press
  ISBN 0-88150-534-X

Resources

Astoria/Warrenton Area
Chamber of Commerce
503-325-6311 / 800-875-6807
www.oldoregon.com

Astoria-Warrenton
Highway 101 Visitor Center
503-861-1031
www.oldoregon.com

Bandon
Chamber of Commerce
541-347-9616
www.bandon.com

Bay Area
Chamber of Commerce
541-269-0215 / 800-824-8486
www.oregonsbayareachamber.com

Brookings-Harbor
Chamber of Commerce
541-469-3181 / 800-535-9469
www.brookingsor.com

Cannon Beach
Chamber of Commerce
503-436-2623
www.cannonbeach.org

Central Oregon
Coast Association
541-265-2064 / 800-767-2064
www.CoastVisitor.com

Charleston
Information Center
541-888-2311 / 800-824-8486

Coos Bay/North Bend Promotions
& Convention & Visitors Bureau
541-269-8921
www.oregonsbayarea.com

Coquille
Chamber of Commerce
541-396-3414
www.coquillechamber.com

Depoe Bay
Chamber of Commerce
541-765-2889 / 877-485-8348
www.depoebaychamber.org

Florence Area
Chamber of Commerce
541-3128 / 800-524-4864
www.florencechamber.com

Garibaldi
Chamber of Commerce
503-322-0301
www.garibaldioregon.com

Greater Gold Beach
Chamber of Commerce
541-247-7526 / 800-525-2334
www.goldbeachchamber.com

Greater Newport
Chamber of Commerce
541-265-8801 / 800-262-7844
www.newportchamber.org

Greater Port Orford/North Curry
Chamber of Commerce
541-332-4101
www.portorfordoregon.com

Lakeside
Chamber of Commerce
541-759-3981
lksdchamber.presys.com

Lincoln City Visitor
Chamber of Commerce
541-994-3070
www.lcchamber.com

Lincoln City Visitor
& Convention Bureau
541-994-8378 / 800-452-2151
www.oregoncoast.org

Myrtle Point
Chamber of Commerce
541-572-5272

Nehalem Bay Area
Chamber of Commerce
503-368-5100 / 877-368-5100
www.nehalembaychamber.com

Nestucca Valley
Chamber of Commerce
503-392-4499
www.cloverdaleoregon.com

Nestucca Valley
Chamber of Commerce
503-392-4499
www.cloverdaleoregon.com

North Bend
Visitor Center
541-756-4613
www.oregonsbayareachamber.com

Oregon Coast
Visitors Association
541-574-2679 / 888-628-2101
www.visittheoregoncoast.com

Oregon Tourism
Commission
800-547-7842
www.traveloregon.com

Reedsport/Winchester
Chamber of Commerce
541271-3495 / 800-247-2155
www.reedsportcc.org

Rockaway Beach
Chamber of Commerce
503-355-8108
www.rockawaybeach.net

Seaside
Visitors Bureau
503-738-3097 / 888-306-2326
www.seasideor.com

Tillamook
Chamber of Commerce
503-842-7525
www.tillamookchamber.org

Toledo
Chamber of Commerce
541-336-3183
www.visittoledooregon.com

Waldport
Chamber of Commerce
541-563-2133
www.waldport-chamber.com

Yachats Area
Chamber of Commerce
541-547-3530 / 800-929-0477
www.yachats.org

Museums

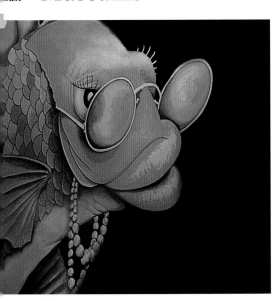

Astoria
Captain George Flavel House
503/325-2203
Columbia River Maritime Museum
503/325-2323
The Heritage Museum
503/325-2203
Uppertown Firefighters Museum
503/325-2203

Bandon
Bandon's Coquille River Museum
541/347-2164

Cannon Beach
Cannon Beach Historical Society
503/436-9301

Coos Bay
Coos Art Museum
541/267-3901
Marshfield Sun Printing Museum
541/267-3762

Florence
Dolls Wares Doll Museum
541/997.3391
Siuslaw Pioneer Museum
541/997-7884

Gold Beach
Curry Historical Museum
541/247-6113

Lincoln City
North Lincoln County Historical Museum
541/996-6614

Myrtle Point
Coos County Logging Museum
541/572-1014

Newport
Hatfield Marine Science Center
541/867-0271
Oregon Coast Aquarium
541/867-3474
Oregon Coast History Center
541/265-7509
Yaquina Bay Lighthouse
541/265-5679

North Bend
Coos County Historical Society Museum
541/756-6320

Oceanside
Friends of Cape Meares Lighthouse & Wildlife Refuge
503/842-5270

Port Orford
Port Orford Lifeboat Station Museum
541/332-0521

Reedsport
Umpqua Discovery Center
541/271-4816

Seaside
Seaside Museum & Historical Society
503/738-7065

Tillamook
Latimer Quilt and Textile Center
503/842-8622
Tillamook Air Museum
503/842-1130
Tillamook County Pioneer Museum
503/842-4553

Toledo
Toledo Historical Museum
541/265-7509

Waldport
Alsea Bay Historic Interpretive Center
541/563-2002
Waldport Heritage Museum
541/563-7092

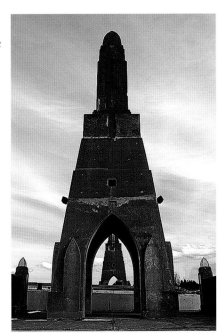

Surf Fisherman on The Sea Wall

He comes striding along the tidal causeway.
He carries a pole and a lure-box by his side.
He climbs and then catwalks the sea wall.
              He throws a cast to the tide.

We wait and watch to see what he is casting to.
We wonder if he will catch a whale or lose his pride.
We look to see how far he heaves the lure.
              He faces a strong incoming tide.

He shows no fear while he is on the wall.
He seems more than willing to risk his hide.
He leaves this perilous perch the way he came.
              He knows he can't outcast the tide.

▲ *This gray cat, resting comfortably in it's own wicker chair, views the world from high up in Astoria's hills filled with old Victorian homes. A true Astorian with the proper attitude.*

Oregon Coast Branch Offices.

Brewster Press

P.O. Box 2356
Wilsonville, OR 97070-2356

Email: brewsterbiz@aol.com
www.brewsterphotos.com